MW01055961

EXHIBITING AT TRADE SHOWS

Susan A. Friedmann

CRISP PUBLICATIONS, INC.
Los Altos, California

EXHIBITING AT TRADE SHOWS

Susan A. Friedmann

CREDITS:
Editor: **Kay Kepler**
Designer: **Carol Harris**
Typesetting: **ExecuStaff**
Cover Design: **Carol Harris**
Artwork: **Ralph Mapson**

Copyright © 1992 Crisp Publications, Inc.
Printed in the United States of America by Bawden Printing Company.

English language Crisp books are distributed worldwide. Our major international distributors include:

CANADA: Reid Publishing, Ltd., Box 69559—109 Thomas St., Oakville, Ontario Canada L6J 7R4. TEL: (416) 842-4428; FAX: (416) 842-9327

AUSTRALIA: Career Builders, P.O. Box 1051, Springwood, Brisbane, Queensland, Australia 4127. TEL: 841-1061, FAX: 841-1580

NEW ZEALAND: Career Builders, P.O. Box 571, Manurewa, Auckland, New Zealand. TEL: 266-5276, FAX: 266-4152

JAPAN: Phoenix Associates Co., Mizuho Bldg. 2-12-2, Kami Osaki, Shinagawa-Ku, Tokyo 141, Japan. TEL: 3-443-7231, FAX: 3-443-7640

Selected Crisp titles are also available in other languages. Contact International Rights Manager Tim Polk at (415) 949-4888 for more information.

Library of Congress Catalog Card Number 91-76243
Friedmann, Susan A.
Exhibiting at Trade Shows
ISBN 1-56052-137-6

This book is printed on recyclable paper with soy ink.

PRINTED WITH SOY INK

TO THE READER

I am continually amazed that so many companies invest thousands of dollars exhibiting at the multitude of trade and consumer shows, conferences, expositions and mall shows that exist in this country, and yet very few organizations seem to take this important marketing vehicle seriously.

Many companies believe that shows last only for a few days, they interfere with the normal selling routine and are often a hindrance to the employees involved in them.

Exhibiting, in reality, is a powerful extension to a company's advertising, promotion, public relations and sales function. Companies are seen by customers, prospects and the general public in unusual ways and can present a broader view of themselves and their activities.

Why then do so many company representatives parade themselves in the public eye displaying body language that appears to say that this is a futile and unimportant exercise, and they would much prefer to be out there in the real world selling?

Many companies fail to share the importance of exhibiting with their employees. Why? Because they are often not convinced of the importance of trade shows in relation to their overall marketing strategy.

When you commit to exhibiting at any type of event you make an investment. As with any other investment, you expect a return. Significant returns come only when wise decisions are made.

This book will help you understand the exciting, challenging and complex trade show arena. It contains numerous easy-to-use and practical ''how-to'' strategies to help you achieve more successful and profitable exhibiting results.

Whether you are a one-person operation or a multinational corporation, exhibit at a trade or consumer show, a conference, exposition or mall show, there is something in here for you. This book is a required survival kit for every exhibitor!

Susan A. Friedmann

i

ACKNOWLEDGMENTS

With special thanks to:

Alec, Dov and Yael, my family, most loyal supporters and best critics, for their never-ending love, enthusiasm and inspiration, without which this book would never have been written.

Bob Kramer for his friendship, support and helpful ideas.

Richard Erschik, Scott Goldman and Paula Marlow, my colleagues and friends, for helping critique and edit the draft of this book.

The seminar participants and colleagues who generously shared their experiences and ideas with me.

ABOUT THE AUTHOR

Susan Friedmann is president of Diadem Communications, based in Cincinnati, Ohio. She has more than 15 years experience as a sales and marketing professional working with commercial, industrial and medical organizations in the United States and in Europe.

She has developed and implemented programs for show organizers, individual companies representing more than 30 industries, associations, chambers of commerce and universities. She has published articles in professional and trade publications and has been a featured speaker at conventions and on radio programs. She is an active member of the National Speakers Association, the Ohio Speakers Forum, the Trade Show Bureau and the American Marketing Association.

CONTENTS

ABOUT THIS BOOK

This book provides an easy-to-follow map for today's exhibitor. It guides you from beginning to end in the most efficient and effective way to exhibit at trade shows. By introducing the basic skills needed, you can become a successful and profitable exhibitor. Through the many helpful suggestions, tips and techniques, you will achieve the results you want from exhibiting.

The book is divided into four sections. Each section supplies down-to-earth information, step-by-step approaches, useful tips and practical guidelines. Planning worksheets help structure your exhibiting practice in advance.

Section I—Planning lays the groundwork for exhibiting, the purpose and the basic information needed to get started.

Section II—Promotion examines promotional opportunities, why they are important and how to integrate them into the overall exhibiting plan.

Section III—People reviews the process of selecting the people to represent the exhibiting company and the skills they need to be effective.

Section IV—Productivity explores after-show follow up to ensure effective results.

Set a goal to select several ideas from this book and put them into practice at your next show. Then integrate more techniques at each following show. Your success will grow from show to show, as you learn what works for your organization.

Be open and creative in adapting the tips and techniques to your own environment. You may need to modify them to fit your unique requirements.

INTRODUCTION

Exhibiting is a component of each of the four main promotional vehicles—advertising, sales promotion, public relations and personal sales. By exhibiting, you are advertising, promoting and selling your company image, products or services.

The Marketing Communications Mix

The Four P's of Exhibit Marketing

This book is divided into four sections, (Planning, Promotion, People and Productivity). These are the four P's of marketing at trade shows.

Trade shows need to have top management's total support and commitment. It is only when management is committed that the right climate and leadership exists—enabling a comprehensive marketing-oriented approach. Top management needs to understand the power of trade shows as they relate to overall company image and future profitability.

Before you begin your future in trade shows, always remember the four P's of exhibit marketing:

✔ **Planning**   ✔ **People**

✔ **Promotion**   ✔ **Productivity**

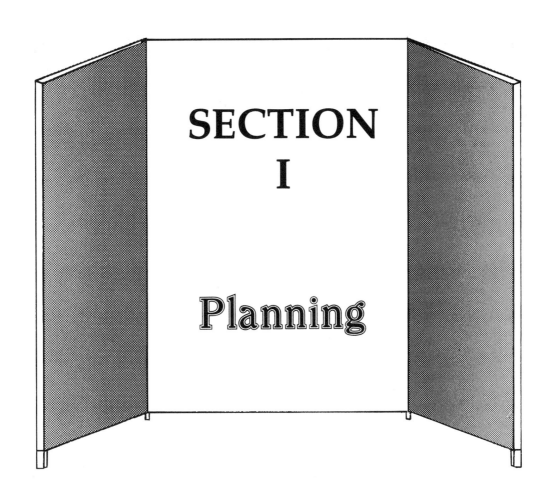

SECTION
I

Planning

PLANNING: STEP 1

Before deciding to exhibit at trade shows, you need to answer the following questions:

▶ *Where do trade shows fit into your marketing strategy?*

▶ *Why is your company exhibiting?*

▶ *What does your company want to exhibit?*

▶ *Who is your target audience (those people you most want to introduce to your products or services)?*

▶ *What is your exhibiting budget?*

Let's examine the importance of each of these questions.

Where do trade shows fit into your marketing strategy?

Examine your present marketing plan and determine how you can best use trade shows to enhance your strategy. Do you want to:

• Increase existing products or services in existing markets
• Introduce new products or services into existing markets
• Introduce existing products or services into new markets
• Introduce new products or services into new markets.

Based on the strategy you choose, you can then determine more specifically . . .

Why is your company exhibiting?

As with any project you undertake, you need to know the reason for doing it. What are your goals? Do you want to:

• Increase sales
• Introduce new products or services
• Enhance your company image
• Educate your target audience
• Recruit dealers or distributors
• Conduct market research.

PLANNING: STEP 1 (continued)

Become a SMART Goal Setter

Whatever your exhibiting goals are, they need to be written down. Always follow the SMART principle

| **S** | Goals need to be written in **Specific** language stating the quality and quantity ·of the results required. |

| **M** | Goals need to be **Measurable.** |

| **A** | Goals need to be **Attainable.** |

| **R** | Goals need to be **Realistic.** |

| **T** | Goals need to have a **Time** frame or deadline. |

Example:

Goal: To generate 50 leads (quantity) from new prospects (quality) for the Mark IV widget, to be converted into 10 sales (quality), by 00/00/0000 (deadline).

Goals formulated in this way can be measured. When you can measure your achievements, you can determine the success of your exhibiting experience.

Bonus Tip: Involve your exhibit staff in goal setting. It makes them more accountable for your company's show results and will increase their enthusiasm for participating.

Setting Your SMART Goals

Goal #1 _____

    Quantity: _____

    Quality: _____

    Deadline: _____

Goal #2 _____

    Quantity: _____

    Quality: _____

    Deadline: _____

Goal #3 _____

    Quantity: _____

    Quality: _____

    Deadline: _____

Control Tip: Always ask yourself: ''Is this goal attainable and realistic?''

PLANNING: STEP 1 (continued)

90 Reasons to Exhibit in an Exposition

Check those that apply to your organization:

- [ ] Demonstrate new products or services
- [ ] Meet buyer face to face
- [ ] Interact with audience preselected by interest
- [ ] Appeal to special customer interests
- [ ] See buyers not usually accessible to sales personnel
- [ ] Uncover unknown buying influences
- [ ] Be compared with other suppliers
- [ ] Showcase technical support personnel
- [ ] Shorten buying process
- [ ] Make immediate sales
- [ ] Project image
- [ ] Create image
- [ ] Continue customer contact
- [ ] Meet potential clients
- [ ] Qualify buyers
- [ ] Introduce new products or services
- [ ] Demonstrate nonportable equipment
- [ ] Understand customer problems
- [ ] Solve customer problems
- [ ] Identify new product or service applications
- [ ] Showcase projected new product or service
- [ ] Obtain product or service feedback
- [ ] Build sales force morale
- [ ] Create dealer network
- [ ] Educate sales force
- [ ] Educate dealers
- [ ] Relate to competition
- [ ] Conduct market research
- [ ] Recruit personnel
- [ ] Attract new representation
- [ ] Highlight new products or services to media
- [ ] Use as three-dimensional sales opportunity
- [ ] Develop action-oriented media
- [ ] Create customer lists
- [ ] Show audio visuals on products or services
- [ ] Support wholesalers
- [ ] Reach customers at low cost per call
- [ ] See top management personnel
- [ ] Meet power buyers
- [ ] Target market by type of attendance
- [ ] Target market by function of attendance
- [ ] Develop leads for dealers
- [ ] Develop leads for wholesalers
- [ ] Develop leads for representatives
- [ ] Reach known prospects not being contacted
- [ ] Reach unknown prospects not being contacted
- [ ] Reach existing customers who need personal attention

- ☐ Diffuse customer complaints
- ☐ Integrate exhibit in total marketing picture
- ☐ Understand customer attitudes
- ☐ Feature product or service benefits
- ☐ Distribute product or service information
- ☐ Conduct sales meetings
- ☐ Create an event or impression
- ☐ Present live product demonstrations
- ☐ Support corporate theme program
- ☐ Invite special customers
- ☐ Introduce new approach to market
- ☐ Introduce new promotional program
- ☐ Introduce a free service
- ☐ Distribute product samples
- ☐ Introduce new selling techniques
- ☐ Program the sales environment
- ☐ Create product laboratory
- ☐ Dramatize your message
- ☐ Create more contacts per sales person in short time period
- ☐ Pinpoint low-cost personal selling opportunity
- ☐ Create high return-on-investment opportunities
- ☐ Introduce company to market

- ☐ Meet customers not normally called upon
- ☐ Encourage 54 percent of sales to be closed without a sales call
- ☐ Reposition your company in a market
- ☐ Change perception of your company
- ☐ Stand above competition
- ☐ Enhance word-of-mouth market
- ☐ Open doors for personal sales calls
- ☐ Reinforce personal sales calls
- ☐ Reinforce direct mail
- ☐ Reduce sales costs
- ☐ Generate qualified leads
- ☐ Generate prospects
- ☐ Make more sales calls
- ☐ Promote multi-services or products for market
- ☐ Promote technical benefits, data or features
- ☐ Promote positive product or service trends
- ☐ Overcome unfavorable publicity
- ☐ Offer product and/or service literature
- ☐ Invite potential customers
- ☐ Support sponsoring organizations
- ☐ Expose new employees to an industry

(Compiled by Donald J. Walter, CEM, Executive Director of National Association of Exposition Managers. Reprinted with permission of NAEM ''Inform-A-Gram,'' #113)

PLANNING: STEP 1 (continued)

What does your company want to exhibit?

Your goals will determine the products or services your company needs to exhibit. For example, if you plan to launch a new product or service, your exhibit needs to focus on the new product.

Often companies with several product lines feel it necessary to display their complete range. This coverage not only demonstrates that no specific goals have been planned, but it is also overwhelming and confusing to the booth visitor, who needs to determine at a glance what business you are in.

What products or services do you plan to exhibit?

Products:

_____

_____

_____

Services:

_____

_____

_____

Who is your target audience?

Which groups would be most interested in your products or services?

- ► Present customers or clients
- ► Specifiers
- ► Suppliers
- ► Influencers
- ► Technical personnel
- ► Manufacturers
- ► Consumers
- ► Others

Who is your target audience? _____

_____

What is your exhibiting budget?

Budgeting Guidelines

Space 24%

Booth expenses (including furnishings and equipment) 33%

Show services (including utilities). 22%

Transportation 13%

Advertising, promotional and special activities 4%

Personnel (including travel, hotel and expenses) 4%

(Source: *Trade Show Bureau Research Report on Cost Analysis, #2060,* August 1988.)

The checklist on page 10 will help you keep a more accurate account of your expenses.

PLANNING: STEP 1 (continued)

Budgeting Checklist

	Estimated	Actual
	Cost	
1. Space		
[ ] Booth	$_____	$_____
[ ] Hotel suite	$_____	$_____
2. Display		
[ ] Design and construction	$_____	$_____
[ ] Graphics	$_____	$_____
[ ] Refurbishing	$_____	$_____
[ ] Products for display	$_____	$_____
[ ] Booth rental	$_____	$_____
[ ] Used booth purchase	$_____	$_____
[ ] Literature holders	$_____	$_____
[ ] Easels	$_____	$_____
[ ] Tool kit	$_____	$_____
[ ] Lighting fixtures	$_____	$_____
3. Furnishing at Booth		
[ ] Tables	$_____	$_____
[ ] Chairs	$_____	$_____
[ ] Ashtrays	$_____	$_____
[ ] Coat racks	$_____	$_____
[ ] Floor covering	$_____	$_____
[ ] Floral arrangements	$_____	$_____
[ ] Computer rental	$_____	$_____
[ ] Imprinter rental	$_____	$_____
[ ] Audiovisual equipment	$_____	$_____
4. Show Services		
[ ] Set-up/Tear-down labor	$_____	$_____
[ ] Electricity	$_____	$_____
[ ] Water, gas, air	$_____	$_____
[ ] Telephone, fax	$_____	$_____
[ ] Booth cleaning	$_____	$_____
[ ] Photos of display	$_____	$_____
[ ] Security	$_____	$_____
[ ] Federal Express	$_____	$_____

	Cost	
	Estimated	Actual

5. Shipping and Storage
[ ]   Freight $_____ $_____
[ ]   Drayage $_____ $_____
[ ]   Exhibit storage $_____ $_____
[ ]   Insurance $_____ $_____

6. Advertising and Promotion
[ ]   Preshow promotion $_____ $_____
[ ]   On-site promotion $_____ $_____
[ ]   Postshow promotion $_____ $_____
[ ]   Direct mail $_____ $_____
[ ]   Special badges $_____ $_____
[ ]   Special uniforms $_____ $_____
[ ]   Handouts, giveaways $_____ $_____
[ ]   Special show literature $_____ $_____
[ ]   Telemarketing $_____ $_____

7. Personnel
[ ]   Travel reservations $_____ $_____
[ ]   Hotel reservations $_____ $_____
[ ]   Registrations at show $_____ $_____
[ ]   Meals $_____ $_____
[ ]   Out-of-pocket expenses $_____ $_____

8. Special Activities
[ ]   Client entertainment $_____ $_____
[ ]   Receptions $_____ $_____
[ ]   Sales meetings $_____ $_____
[ ]   Speakers, training $_____ $_____

9. Other
[ ]   _____ $_____ $_____
[ ]   _____ $_____ $_____
[ ]   _____ $_____ $_____
[ ]   _____ $_____ $_____

Total Show Budget $_____ $_____

PLANNING: STEP 1 (continued)

Choosing the Right Shows

Your company could be represented at many kinds of shows, including international, national, regional and local exhibitions.

International shows are often major events, which attract exhibitors and attendees from all corners of the globe. These shows offer a forum for launching new products and discussing industry issues. In the United States, these events typically attract 20 percent of their participants from overseas.

National shows are primarily targeted to buyers and sellers in a specialized industry and are promoted to attract visitors nationwide. Frequently though, many of the attendees come from a 200–300 mile radius.

Regional shows are organized in a particular area of the country and attract visitors from a 200 mile radius. State shows are included in this category. Many of these events are open to the public.

Local shows draw attendance from the immediate vicinity and are often open to the trade and the general public. They include consumer shows such as home shows, hobby shows or boating shows, which specifically attract many local attendees.

Before you choose a show to attend, ask yourself:

- Which show best fits our needs? It should be within your budget, in a serviceable location, and it should occur at a convenient time and attract your target audience.

- Where is the show located? If your company services a specific area of the country, you should attend shows that draw only from that region. If you want to expand your market into new areas, you need to investigate shows that attract prospects from those areas. According to trade show research, national shows draw 40 percent of their attendees from within a 200 mile radius of the site.

- How successful has this show been in the past?

- How is the show promoted?

Resources for Show Information

► Trade show directories

► Trade show magazines

► Trade and professional associations

► Trade and professional publications

► Chambers of commerce

► World trade centers

► Customers

► Suppliers

► Competitors

PLANNING: STEP 2

The next step in your planning is to consider items such as: space requirements, space location, booth display, show regulations, and transportation. We will look at each individually.

1. Determine How Much Exhibit Space You Need

Your goals and budget are the primary determining factors on space. Some companies, however, want to make a statement about their size in the market and will buy space accordingly.

Space is normally sold in multiples of 10 square feet, with the standard space being 10' × 10'. The larger and more prestigious the show, the higher square footage is likely to be priced.

What you plan to exhibit will also have a bearing on the size space needed. If you intend to demonstrate a large piece of equipment, you need enough room for those involved in the demonstration, including onlookers.

> **Bonus Tip:** For your first appearance at a particular show, consider a standard 10' × 10' space to test the environment.

2. Where Your Space Should Be Located

Every company wants the ideal location. However, every show is different and what is perfect for one will differ for another.

Two guiding principles are to position your booth to the right of the entrance or the central area on the show floor. People tend to gravitate to the right or to the center.

If the show you attend is in the same location every year, study the traffic patterns and then choose your booth accordingly.

Many exhibitors avoid restroom and food stations. However, some exhibitors get an excellent response from these areas.

Before making any final decisions, discuss the floor layout with show management to determine where the main attractions, industry leaders and competitors are situated. Then decide how close you want to be to them.

Areas to Avoid

1. Columns that obstruct	6. Freight doors
2. Low ceilings	7. Dark spaces
3. Restrooms	8. Rear exits
4. Food stations	9. Seminar sites
5. Dead-end aisles	10. Competitors

Bonus Tip: Avoid companies that demonstrate noisy equipment or have crowd-drawing attractions. Check with show management beforehand.

3. Your Booth Display

The many displays on the market broadly fit into two main categories: portable systems and custom-built displays. Standard portable systems include:

- Table tops
- Panel systems
- Pop-up systems
- Modular systems
- Graphic panel displays.

Depending on the manufacturer, these can be built to your color specifications. Custom-built displays are designed and constructed to showcase your products or services in a more sensational manner.

PLANNING: STEP 2 (continued)

Basic Guidelines

1. Budget.

Your budget will dictate the type, size and make of display you can mount and the amount of space you reserve.

2. Image.

Do you want to portray yourself as quality, high-tech, established, contemporary, sporty or traditional? Shape, color and design will help to create the image of your choice.

3. Show frequency.

If you exhibit at several shows each year, consider the display's ability to survive the harsh handling often experienced during transportation.

4. Flexibility and versatility.

Consider your needs for different set-up configurations from show to show and growth potential for future display additions. For example, you can choose a model that serves both as a floor model and a table-top display.

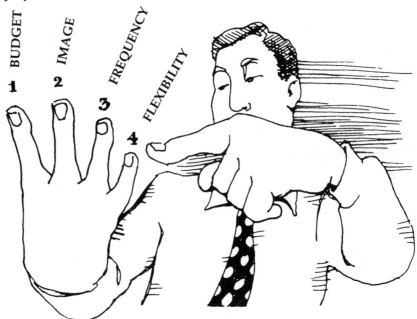

Questions to Ask

Who will set up and tear down the exhibit?

In addition to budgetary constraints, knowing who will set up and dismantle your exhibit—unions, show contractors, or your own personnel—can be an important factor in your selection decision.

How easy is it to set up and dismantle the exhibit?

How many parts and pieces does the exhibit require? Fewer parts can mean quicker and easier installation and tear down. In addition, the quicker your exhibit can be installed, the less it costs when union labor needs to be hired.

What and how will products be displayed?

How does the exhibit meet your needs for displaying products and do you have any special requirements? Consider your needs for shelving, special graphics or effects, demonstration areas.

What further logistical information is needed?

Pay special attention to what services need to be ordered, including electricity, water, drainage; labor and drayage rates (rates for taking and storing your containers from the shipping dock to your space on the exhibit floor) and show rules and regulations. Remember that show management is there to help you. When in doubt, ask.

Bonus Tip: Consider renting a booth if you are exhibiting for the first time and are unsure of this marketing medium. Many of the display manufacturers have rental or rent-to-buy programs.

(Source for booth display information: Michael J. Scherer, Downing Displays, Inc. Cincinnati, OH.)

PLANNING: STEP 2 (continued)

Does Your Booth Pass the Three-Second Test?

To be effective, your booth needs to pass the Three-Second Test. In three seconds, a visitor needs to be able to:

- Notice your booth. It needs to be striking enough to grab their attention. Color and lights, special effects, life-size or larger-than-life graphics, banners or flags, moving objects, mirrors, mannequins, robots and active demonstrations will all grab visitors' attention.

- Establish your identity by a distinctive logo or your company name. If your company logo is well-known, make it conspicuous. Similarly, make your company name noticeable and legible.

- Determine what benefit your product or service is to the consumer. Use benefit statements that can be easily read and understood on graphic panels, headers and so on. Each statement needs to start with ''How to . . .'' For example, ''How to be in 10 places at once without having to leave your office.''

Bonus Tip: You need to emphasize company or brand identification in a national trade show and product identification in a consumer show.

4. What Are the Show Regulations?

Each show has its own restrictions. All the information you need is usually in the exhibitor show manual. The presentation of this material varies quite considerably. The trend is to simplify it for the exhibitor as much as possible.

Listed in the manual should be the following: show schedules, rules and regulations, exhibit policy, a floor plan, exhibit specifications, show service order forms, registration information, shipping and advertising or promotional details.

5. What Type of Transportation Is Needed?

Shape, size and weight of your display govern whether your display is transported by car, van, truck or plane. Knowing the transportation requirements beforehand will help to determine the most economical means of shipping available.

Usually the show has an official freight-handling contractor. This company is normally extremely knowledgeable about the show, the facilities and handling exhibit systems. Although it is recommended, you are not obligated to use this company, but do make sure that the contractor you choose is reputable and has convention and exhibit experience.

Bonus Tip: Know the weight of each shipping case both empty and full, so you can check that the contractor and drayage company are charging you for the correct weight.

Exhibiting at Trade Shows

PLANNING: STEP 2 (continued)

Working with Union Labor

Avoid any unnecessary difficulties when you work with contract or union labor. A few guidelines will keep everything running smoothly.

1. Treat labor civilly. They are there to do a job and unless they are harassed, they will usually perform satisfactorily.

2. Allow the workers to do their job their way, which is not always the same way you might do the job.

3. Any problems need to be reported to the union steward or show management. They are usually more effective in handling problems than you.

4. Know the show rules and regulations that apply to union labor. This information is found in the exhibitor manual. Be aware that rules vary for every show.

5. Arrange for the same team to install and dismantle your exhibit. It will save time since they will already be familiar with your display.

6. Have everything you need ready before engaging your union team. Remember that they are on a meter and every wasted minute is costing you money.

7. Check the union rates and, as far as possible, avoid using union labor after regular work hours and on weekends. Their rates are double at these times.

Bonus Tip: Treat others as you would want to be treated, irrespective of their position.

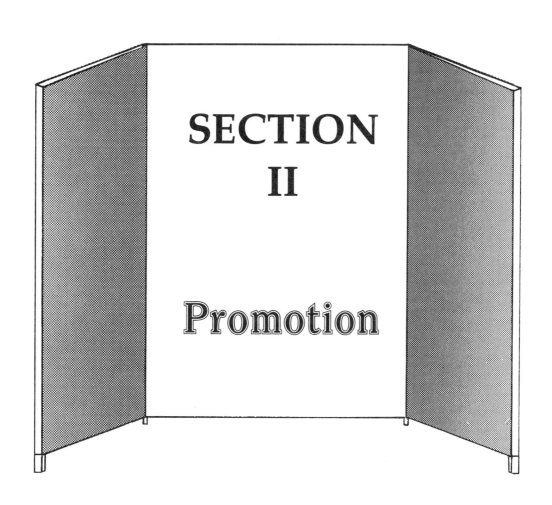

SECTION
II

Promotion

PROMOTION

Many companies believe that show management is totally responsible for attracting people to the show and ultimately to their booth. A poor attendance at their booth results in bitter complaints to show management.

The truth is that show management is responsible only for promoting the show to the right target audience. It is accountable to exhibitors for delivering quality traffic to the show. What visitors do once they are at the show is no longer under show management's control.

It is the exhibitor's responsibility to inform their prime target market what they will be exhibiting, where they will be located in the show hall and why they should visit your display.

This promotion is becoming more important as trade show visitors have less time available for shows. According to industry research, 76 percent of show attendees come with a fixed agenda. If they are not aware of your participation ahead of time, they may not find your booth or even be interested in stopping.

PROMOTION (continued)

What can be done to encourage attendees to visit your booth? The goals and target audience established in your planning stage are the nucleus for your promotional strategy. The five main promotion vehicles available to generate booth traffic are:

1. PERSONAL INVITATIONS

2. TELEMARKETING

3. DIRECT MAIL

4. ADVERTISING

5. PUBLIC RELATIONS

Trade show industry studies show you can increase visitation to a booth by as much as 33 percent as a result of a coordinated preshow promotion by the exhibitor.

How Do Customers Learn about Trade Shows?

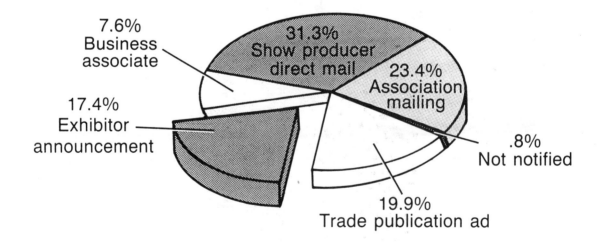

(Source: Trade Show Bureau, Denver, Co.)

GENERATING BOOTH TRAFFIC

Personal Invitations

This strategy is best when extended to a special and select group; for example, key customers or prospects. It may also carry more influence when top management issues the invitation.

Show management often offers complimentary or discounted tickets, which can be distributed along with your personal invitation.

> **Bonus Tip:** If your guest is driving to the show, investigate the possibility of prepaying their parking.

Telemarketing

This strategy is used for setting specific booth appointments and is an alternative way of issuing personal invitations.

It is essential that the telemarketer be well scripted, extremely professional and enthusiastic. To entice the prospective visitor to your booth, the script needs to be benefit-oriented. Ask yourself what your products or services do for your visitor: save time, save money or increase productivity.

Direct Mail

Your direct mail campaign needs to have a specific purpose based on your show goals and objectives. What action do you want recipients to take once they receive your mailing? For example, should they come to your booth to:

- Participate in a contest
- Collect a gift
- See a demonstration.

Whatever your reason, it is also important to measure the effectiveness of your campaign. Keep track of these respondents by requiring people to return a coupon or questionnaire in exchange for a gift.

GENERATING BOOTH TRAFFIC (continued)

An effective mailing campaign needs a minimum of three pieces released at planned intervals. Differentiate your mailing from the others.

Direct Mail Tips

- Use a qualified mailing list
- Use first-class mail
- Address mailing to an individual
- Purchase interesting-looking postage stamps
- Have a postage meter imprinted with your booth number and show name
- Have envelopes printed with a special message or teaser
- Use odd-sized promotional pieces

- Use bold colors (stock or ink)
- Use a theme
- Create a three-part mailing
- Keep your message short, sweet and simple
- Consider different mailings for different target audiences
- Enclose promotional piece in everything you send out (such as invoices)
- Use color postcards—people always read them!

Guidelines for Developing a Mailing Campaign

► Establish a timeline for your campaign
► Refer to your show goals
► Define your target audience
► Specify what interests your target audience
► Clarify your differentiation from your competitors
► Develop a benefit-oriented message
► Create pre- and postshow promotional pieces
► Include an incentive to visit your booth
► Use small, highly targeted mailings
► Design tracking or evaluation system

Bonus Tip: For optimum exposure, mail three different pieces at two-week intervals beginning seven to eight weeks before the show.

Advertising

Advertising is an important aspect of the promotional mix that can be used to do many things, such as:

- Create awareness or interest

- Transmit information

- Encourage understanding

- Alter perceptions or attitudes

- Differentiate

- Direct actions

- Provide reassurance

- Remind

- Give reasons for buying

- Generate inquiries.

Ultimately, its role is to sell your products or services.

The primary purpose of advertising your participation at a trade or consumer show is to persuade attendees to visit your booth. To create this appeal, your message needs to CHARM:

C   **Convince** visitors your product or service is beneficial

H   **Help** save time and money

A   **Appeal** to attendees' emotions or needs

R   **Reward** their actions

M   Be **Memorable**

GENERATING BOOTH TRAFFIC (continued)

Key Advertising Components

Your promotional budget and your show goals are the key components of your advertising campaign. The budget ascertains the media format you can use, and the show goals lay the foundation for creating specific advertising objectives. For example:

1. Develop or support a distinctive impression of your organization

2. Maintain contact with major target groups

3. Show your organization's capabilities

4. Generate inquiries for more information

5. Obtain feedback for evaluating future strategies

6. Recruit personnel

Your advertising goals then direct the content and placement of your message.

Where Can You Advertise?

Before the show, you can advertise in trade or industry publications, association newsletters, local publications, radio or television outlets, billboards or transit advertising. Use show logos or decals wherever possible, such as on all correspondence. Have company calendars printed with show dates marked to give or send to customers. Produce a special postage meter imprint for the show. Be creative!

At the show, your advertising vehicles could include show catalogs, daily show publications, airport billboards or electronic message boards, city billboards, pocket planners (such as city maps or guides), taxicabs, transit advertising, hotel closed-circuit TV, hotel on- or under-room door promotion, kiosks, billboards or electronic message boards in show hall or balloons.

Bonus Tip: Explore piggyback or cross-promotional opportunities in which you can combine your product or service with another exhibitor's. For example, if you offer computer services to a specific industry, create a campaign with another industry supplier offering a special show price for a joint package. Both of you can then display the package, creating extra exposure.

Organizing Your Advertising Campaign

The following six steps need to be considered when developing your advertising campaign.

1. **Whom are you targeting?**

Always keep in mind the group you are targeting with your message.

Our target audience:

_____

_____

_____

_____

2. **What is your message?**

Do you want to introduce your target group to a new product or service or a new application for an existing product or service? Will you be demonstrating a special piece of equipment?

What would excite your customer to visit your booth? Keep your message short and simple. Concentrate on the benefits and eliminate unnecessary words. Use bold lettering for emphasis.

Our message is:

_____

_____

_____

_____

> **Bonus Tip:** To save money and for faster identification, use an existing advertisement. Add a banner on the top-right with a message such as, ''Come and see us at Booth 123 at the Business Expo.''

GENERATING BOOTH TRAFFIC (continued)

3. Where will it appear?

Which communication media format would best deliver your message?

The best media format for us to use:

Format 1: _____

Format 2: _____

Format 3: _____

4. When will it appear?

If you plan to use trade publications, check their media schedule for advertising deadlines. Trade publications often plan their issues several weeks or months in advance.

Planning is critical for some of the special media formats such as billboards, kiosks or transit advertising, since they are often reserved several months or even years (for large shows) in advance.

Deadlines for advertising:

Format 1: _____

Format 2: _____

Format 3: _____

5. How much money is available for advertising?

What is a realistic advertising budget that will achieve your goals?

Our advertising budget:

Format 1: _____

Format 2: _____

Format 3: _____

6. How will you measure your results?

Will you have visitors bring the advertisement to the booth in exchange for a gift or discount coupon or ask visitors where they saw your advertisement?

Our tracking and evaluation system: _____

_____

Public Relations

Public relations should enhance the reputation of a product, service or a company in the eyes of the public. Its effect before and at a show can increase the number of visitors to your display, as well as supply information to people who cannot or will not attend the event.

Advertising is different from public relations. Advertising persuades people to buy or take some desired action on your products or services. Public relations attempts to generate knowledge, understanding, confidence and goodwill.

To be effective, your trade show public relations effort needs to coincide with your advertising goals. PR's primary function is to:

- Build awareness

- Enhance your company image

- Educate customers or prospects

- Change opinions.

Types of Trade Show PR Communications

Before the show, your public relations effort should include press releases for local and trade publications, product or service application articles, personal invitations to trade or local editors and company newsletters.

Bonus Tip: Target publications or other media that plan to cover the show. Show management can supply this information.

At the show, your PR efforts should include press kits for the press office, press reception (best used for product launches), videotape or slide and tape presentations at the booth, reprints of PR articles as giveaways, seminars or workshops and using effective booth staff.

GENERATING BOOTH TRAFFIC (continued)

Writing a Press Release

When writing a press release, include the following in a concise format, preferably one typed, double-spaced page.

► *Who*—the publics or audiences

► *What*—the messages to be conveyed

► *Why*—the goals and objectives

► *Where*—the place

► *When*—the schedule or time-frame

► *How*—the techniques used; the evaluation process

► *How much*—the budget or resources

Bonus Tip: Use a human interest story, unusual use of your product or service or a survey to attract a journalist's attention.

What to Include in a Press Kit

Press kits are an important tool to provide journalists with in-depth information about your company, products or services. Always include in your kit the major news announcement (include your booth number in the release) and a supporting black-and-white (5″ × 7″) photograph, if applicable. If you include a photo, do not send a photo of the CEO, liven up a static shot with people and caption all photos. Also include in your press kit a fact sheet consisting of general information, facts and figures about the relevant market and the contact name and phone number for postshow follow-up interviews.

Additional information for a more comprehensive kit can include background notes about your company, existing product or service range, technical details, and so on; product or corporate brochures, if applicable; a question and answer sheet; specific material for television or radio such as video and audio tapes and details of further supporting material such as interview opportunities.

Bonus Tip: Keep your press kits simple. Elaborate folders do not impress journalists. They are only interested in newsworthy and useful information for their readers. Print your company name on the cover to help journalists find your information quickly.

SEMINARS AND WORKSHOPS

Most trade shows have a seminar or workshop section in addition to the exhibit area. At some events, the seminar or workshop program may be the main attraction, and the displays are an added benefit.

If your organization has a representative who can speak well and share practical or useful industry- or product-related information, investigate seminar participation. This form of PR can generate enormous credibility and additional exposure for your company.

Seminar participation should not be used as a promotional platform for your products or services. People who attend these sessions expect valuable information. Their response to blatant promotion is often extremely negative.

HANDOUTS

Picture the show visitors trudging down the aisles laden with plastic carrybags overflowing with material. People visiting shows have a psychological urge to take either whatever is handed to them or what is available to be taken.

With the best will in the world, people may want to read your material. However, the reality is that when they get back to their hotel room, they realize they do not want or need much of the material taken. According to a recent *Wall Street Journal* survey, 75 percent of all literature gathered at shows is discarded before attendees leave the show site. Is yours going to be among the 25 percent of the information that is kept? Why take the chance? Here are some guidelines for managing your handout material.

1. Don't hand out anything expensive. Since you are not sure if your prospect will keep what you hand out, do not hand out your most expensive information. If you want your prospect to leave with something, have inexpensive product sheets developed.

2. Offer to send information. Many prospects will appreciate your offer to send them brochures. This frees them from having to lug around extraneous material and also find room for it in their baggage. However, if you promise to mail your information, do so promptly, because if you don't, your competition will. Consider using overnight mail for ''hot'' prospects.

3. Only give to qualified prospects. Unless your goal is to get some information into as many visitors' hands as possible, make sure that you hand material or offer to send material only to qualified prospects. This avoids giving information to people who are likely to discard it or letting the competition obtain details too easily.

4. Literature does not sell—people do. Randomly handing out information is a barrier to opening up a conversation with a visitor. Often booth staff who feel uncomfortable in the trade show environment will hand things out thinking that they are doing something productive.

The truth is that it is your people who do the selling; your literature acts purely as a back-up. This is one of the reasons why people selection is so important.

> **Bonus Tip:** Consider handing out audio tapes describing your product or service. Attendees would be reluctant to throw a tape away. If you are in the computer industry, hand out important information on floppy disks.

PREMIUMS OR GIVEAWAYS

According to the Specialty Advertising Association International (SAAI), "Giveaways are useful articles imprinted with an advertiser's message and distributed without obligation to the recipient. They are used for communication, motivation, promotion and recognition."

An important aspect of giveaways is to increase your memorability with your customers and booth visitors. Be sure that your giveaway is practical and that it has the company name and phone number on it. Tie your giveaway to your target audience and to any slogan your advertising campaign uses. Finally, use the giveaway as a reward—give it to people who answer your questions, enter your contest, or sign your mailing list.

Use Premiums to Prequalify

Premiums can be used to prequalify your prospects. One company uses playing cards. Prior to the show, they send "kings" to their hottest prospects, "queens" to suppliers, "jacks" to new prospects, and so on. They request that the cards are brought to the booth in exchange for a special gift. When the cards are presented, the booth staff already know certain particulars about their visitor. They can then act on their previous knowledge.

Bonus Tip: Consider handing out a discount coupon or a gift certificate that requires future contact with your company for redemption. This can also help zero in on prospects.

MEASURE YOUR SUCCESS

Establishing a Premium Plan

To measure the success of your giveaway item, you need to establish a plan.

1. What is your budget?

   _____

   _____

2. What do you want to achieve by giving away a premium?

   _____

   _____

3. Whom do you want to receive your premium?

   _____

   _____

4. What promotional message do you want to convey to your target?

   _____

   _____

5. What is the best premium to communicate your message?

   _____

   _____

6. How will you inform your target about your giveaway item?

   _____

   _____

7. How will you monitor the results of your promotion?

   _____

   _____

CASE STUDIES

(The following case studies are reprinted courtesy of the Specialty Advertising Association International.)

Company: Harris Calorific

Objective: To build trade show traffic in order to recruit distributors.

Strategy: Convinced that it could build its distributor network if its salespeople could spend a few minutes talking with prospective dealers, the advertiser mailed executive desk folders to 240 selected dealers. This was accompanied by a reprint of the firm's trade magazine advertising and a letter from the vice president inviting recipients to visit the Harris booth at the American Welding Society's trade show. The folder's vinyl cover was embossed "Respected for quality," the corporate slogan. A small recess with imprinting was the only purely commercial aspect of the cover. The hot-stamped information invited recipients to come by the booth where they could obtain a personalized nameplate to place over the recess and give the folder the finishing touch. The nameplates were also delivered by salespeople to distributors who didn't attend the show.

Result: At the trade show, 63 percent of the targeted distributors visited the Harris booth to pick up their personalized nameplates. Against a norm of five to seven leads, the promotion generated 25 concrete leads for new distributors.

Company: 3M Telcomm Products Division

Objective: To motivate trade show registrants to visit all units of an exhibitor's display area.

Strategy: A manufacturer of telephone equipment and supplies, composed of seven groups, planned to combine its seven exhibits in one display tent at a convention. The advertiser wanted registrants to visit each unit of the exhibit. Since the show was being held in Missouri, near the point of origin of the old Pony Express, a promotion using the Pony Express theme was conceived. Some 6,000 potential show attendees were mailed a theme folder containing a replica of an Old West coin and inviting them to visit the exhibit. When registrants came to the Telcomm tent, they were issued a "trail map" with display stations depicted as 1860 Pony Express stops and a Pony Express shopping bag for product literature. They were instructed to visit each stop, where their maps would be stamped. Those completing the "trail ride" could turn in their stamped maps to the "paymaster's window" at the exhibit exit and receive their "pay envelope." The envelopes contained replicas of two gold coins minted in the 1850s and "surprise" gift vouchers, redeemable for merchandise awards.

Results: An estimated 6,000 persons completed the entire "trail ride," 40 percent higher than for a previous show. Sales reps indicated that many new sales opportunities were created as a direct result of the promotional attraction.

CONTESTS

Unless you are planning to develop a mailing list, avoid contests that just involve placing a business card in a box or bowl for a drawing. Think about what you will do with the hundreds of cold business cards after the show. Who will determine whether they are real prospects?

Far more effective is having a mini-questionnaire (three to five questions) as the entry, requesting information from the prospect. Or better still, a contest involving a challenge to the visitor. This gives booth staffers an opportunity to pose qualifying questions. It is important that staffers understand the purpose of the contest. Emphasize that the focus is on qualifying the visitor. The game is merely a means to attract visitors. Far too often, booth personnel concentrate on the winning or losing aspects of the game, forgetting to probe for product or service interest.

Try something a little different: charge the visitor to enter your contest or to fill in a registration form. Let them know that the money will be donated to charity.

> **Bonus Tip:** When organizing a contest, remember to check the state lottery laws.

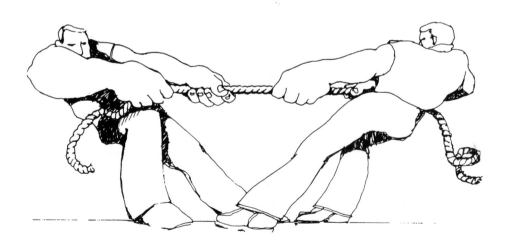

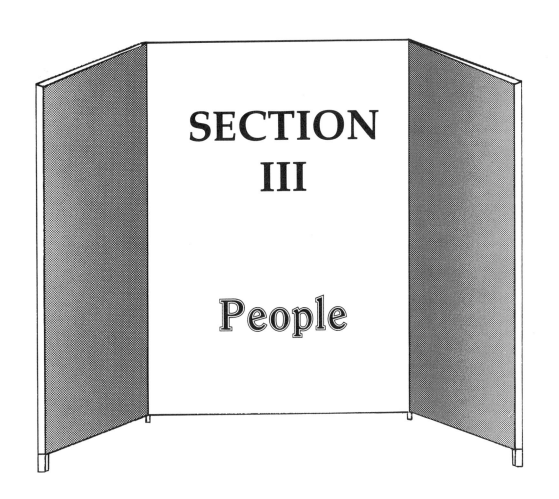

SECTION
III

People

PEOPLE

You have probably visited several trade shows and been exposed to booths staffed by people who either did not want to be there or did not know what they were doing.

The most crucial aspect of any booth is its people. Your image does not stop with an elaborate booth, fancy advertising or impressive literature. These certainly help, but it is people who sell your company and its products or services. The personnel you choose to represent you are your ambassadors. These people have the responsibility of making or breaking future relationships with attendees, prospects and customers.

A study conducted by Allen Konopacki of Incomm Research revealed that 32 percent of attendees did not make a purchase from an exhibitor because of one or more problems with a booth salesperson—the representative did not listen to the prospect's needs, no one was available to assist the visitor, no one followed up after the show, or the prospect did not trust the salesperson.

PEOPLE SELECTION

Use the PEOPLE Formula to Staff Your Booth

Selecting the right personnel to represent your organization is critical to the result expected from your show participation. The PEOPLE formula is an easy way to help you make the best choice.

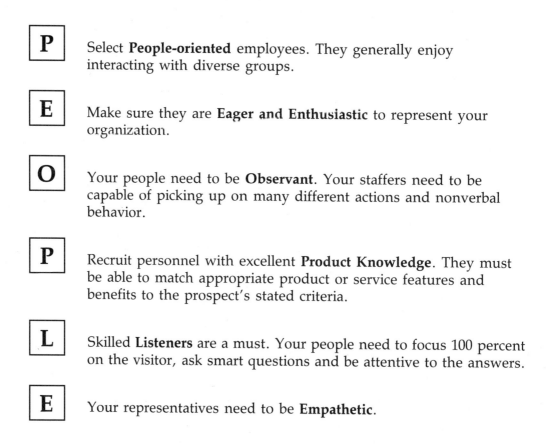

P — Select **People-oriented** employees. They generally enjoy interacting with diverse groups.

E — Make sure they are **Eager and Enthusiastic** to represent your organization.

O — Your people need to be **Observant**. Your staffers need to be capable of picking up on many different actions and nonverbal behavior.

P — Recruit personnel with excellent **Product Knowledge**. They must be able to match appropriate product or service features and benefits to the prospect's stated criteria.

L — Skilled **Listeners** are a must. Your people need to focus 100 percent on the visitor, ask smart questions and be attentive to the answers.

E — Your representatives need to be **Empathetic**.

Bonus Tip: Never offer employees a position in your booth or a trip to the show as a reward. They may not perceive this token in the same way as you do.

Other Staff Criteria

Every trade show attracts distinctive markets and diverse groups of people. A powerful and effective strategy is to have different teams for each show you participate in. For smaller companies this is not always possible. However, an awareness and appreciation of the various groups and their individual needs is beneficial.

According to the H.R. Chally Group and their book, *The Quadrant Solution* (Amacom, 1990) there are four product or market environments:

- New or unique products or services

- High- or new-tech product or service systems

- Accepted and widely used products or services for customers' existing systems

- Commodities.

Each of these environments has different needs and requires different selling skills. It is normal that some people are better suited for some environments than others.

STAFFING FOR THE QUADRANT

STAFFING FOR THE QUADRANT

	New or Unique Products or Services *(trends: laser disc video, high-definition television, laser medical equipment, automotive navigational systems)*	High- or New-Tech Product or Service Systems *(automated processing systems, robotics, just-in-time delivery systems, integrated marketing)*
Prospect Reactions	Buy emotionally or on speculation Often accept a high degree of risk	Lack of expertise with complex systems Question potential "interruption to business" to change to new approach
Prospect Wants or Needs	Ego enhancement Novel or revolutionary design Simple installation and use Performance increase tied to uniqueness Competitive edge Emotional push	Knowledge Customized design Flexibility in features and options Expandability Performance improvement over standard or present system Installation, training and service Initial pilots to hedge risks
Staffer Skills Needed	Positive attitude and high self-confidence Enthusiasm Theatrical demonstration capability Ability to generate excitement Technically knowledgeable Good qualifier	Patience Consultative approach and image Relationship building Expert technical knowledge or credibility Prove company competent to design tailored solutions Team-oriented approach Demonstrate key concepts Handle objections Good communication skills

Accepted and Widely Used Products or Services *(photocopiers, meeting facilities, business forms, fine paper)*	**Commodities** *(office supplies, food, no-load mutual funds)*
Buying complex but standardized products or services Have internal expertise Does it match current standards Looking for best provider of quality or service	Buying standardized products or services Looking for best provider of price and convenience Know what they want Want what they know
Standardized design with flexibility in features and options Match with existing technical specifications On-time delivery Performance improvement over standard systems Some cost savings Repeatable performance Understandable technology	Low cost Easy replacement On-time delivery Ready availability when needed Incentives Consistent quality
Exemplify dependability Show product or service capabilities Build relationships Emphasize customer satisfaction, advocacy Friendly, caring Strive for sales and service leadership Anticipates and prevents problems	Responsive to customer needs Encourage repeat business Basic product information Stress flexible feature and option packaging Show price advantage Emphasize convenience and ease or purchase and delivery Communicate product availability

BOOTH CONTROL

For maximum productivity, your staff should be working on a two-hours-on, two-hours-off schedule. However, this is not always possible due to the number of people you have available to work the booth. The main point is to have organized breaks. Be sure to have a contingency plan for extra booth staff in case of sickness or emergencies.

Small Exhibitors

Small exhibitors who exhibit single-handedly need to consider employing a temporary worker to staff the booth for short periods. Everyone needs a break occasionally. This person need not necessarily be familiar with your products or services, but they could alert interested visitors that you will be available shortly. Or you could train them to obtain some pertinent information for postshow follow up. The important point is that your booth is never left unattended.

SAMPLE BOOTH SCHEDULE →

Booth Schedule

SHOW: _____

CITY: _____

Representative	Function	Date _____		Date _____	
		On	Off	On	Off

BOOTH CONTROL (continued)

What to Do During Breaks

During the breaks encourage your representatives to spend some of their free time walking outside the show environment. Walking is a great energy booster. If you want your team to take advantage of seminars or workshops or visit other displays, plan enough time for them to do this as well as have some free time of their own.

To Feel Better During Shows

1. Drink plenty of water rather than coffee, tea or soft drinks.

2. Eat well-balanced meals low in sugar, caffeine and salt to keep your energy at a more consistent level for longer periods of time.

3. If you must drink coffee or smoke, take multivitamins with a high B-vitamin content for extra stamina and vitality.

4. Get plenty of sleep.

5. Avoid alcohol at all times during show hours and keep it to a minimum after hours.

Bonus Tip: Bring your own ice water cooler so you can keep your throat lubricated.

Avoiding Aches and Pains

When you stand for hours at a time, leg muscles and ligaments contract and tighten, causing painful feet and legs and feelings of fatigue.

Pamper your feet. Wear comfortable, flexible, well-fitting—preferably leather—shoes with arch supports. These will help give your feet more staying power. Socks for men should be made of cotton or wool fibers. Women should wear low-heeled leather pumps.

Avoid high heels and new shoes. They may look nice but they are more likely to give you foot and leg cramps, blisters, soreness and lower back pain.

Take advantage of slow periods during the show to do some of the following simple exercises to stimulate the blood flow in the legs and feet, combat fatigue and ease any minor aches and pains.

BOOTH CONTROL (continued)

Revitalizing Exercises

1. Standing on your right foot, raise the left foot a few inches off the ground and rotate the ankle slowly 5 to 10 times, first in a clockwise and then counterclockwise direction. Repeat with the other foot.

2. Standing on your left foot, raise the right foot a few inches off the ground and move the foot from side to side, in a waving motion. Repeat several times and then switch feet.

3. Standing on your left foot, raise the right foot a few inches off the ground and point the foot upward and then downward several times in slow motion. Repeat with the other foot.

4. Alternate standing on the ball of your right foot to standing on the ball of your left foot. Do this several times in slow motion.

5. Standing with both feet flat on the ground, comfortably apart, gently bend and straighten both knees several times.

6. Standing straight, with arms relaxed at the side of your body, take a slow deep breath in, to the count of five, expanding the diaphragm. Then exhale to the count of five, contracting the diaphragm. Repeat this exercise three to six times.

7. Standing straight, rotate the shoulders 5 to 10 times in a forward and then backward slow motion.

Bonus Tip: Put padded or liquid gel insoles in your shoes to cushion the foot, giving a softer and more comfortable tread, especially on concrete floors. Talcum powder or foot powder will absorb moisture and cool and soothe your feet.

INTERPERSONAL COMMUNICATION SKILLS

Once you have chosen a suitable team to represent your organization, it is important to connect and involve them in every aspect of your exhibiting plans. Communication is one of the keys to success at trade shows. The more your representatives are included, the more accountable and motivated they will be toward the show's success.

To increase motivation involve them in the following areas:

- Exhibiting and individual goal setting

- Promotional campaigns

- At-show expectations

- Postshow evaluation

- Postshow productivity.

It is essential to pass on the following information to your representatives:

1. Why you are exhibiting

The purpose for your organization's involvement in the show and what you are expecting to achieve through your participation.

2. What you are exhibiting

The specific products or services you plan to exhibit. There should be no surprises for your team when they arrive at the booth.

3. What you expect from them

The team needs to be encouraged to set their own goals based on the overall exhibiting goals. They also need to know what you want them to be doing on a daily basis; for example, how many people you expect them to interact with and what kind of information you want.

4. How to do what you expect from them

Train your representatives to be more effective on the show floor. Show them how to demonstrate the products on display or qualify prospects effectively.

INTERPERSONAL COMMUNICATION SKILLS (continued)

Preshow Training

To ensure that your staff have the skills they need, organize an exhibit training session for them. Either use a knowledgeable employee or hire a specialist to do this for you.

Meet with your booth staffers at regular intervals, before the show begins and then at the end of each day, to keep everyone on track. Remind them of what needs to be accomplished, evaluating performance, answering questions, monitoring goals and generally motivating everyone.

It is important to take a few minutes at the end of each day to address some of these matters while they are still fresh in peoples' minds. In addition, it allows you time to handle difficulties before the show opens on the following day.

Motivate with Incentives

In addition to involving your booth staff in the show planning process and encouraging them to set their own goals, consider having an incentive program to create further enthusiasm.

Think about offering one or more of the following:

- Commission on final sales

- Trip

- Recognition award

- Gift certificate (dinner, store, entertainment)

- Time off

- Personal growth or educational seminar.

ON THE SHOW FLOOR

Your team's real skill is put to the test once they are on the show floor. This is where they can either make or break any future business relationship. Their verbal and nonverbal messages are constantly evaluated, either consciously or subconsciously. According to recent research conducted by Allen Konopacki, Incomm Research, 56 percent of a visitor's impression is determined in the first three or four seconds.

Dress

It is important that your people look presentable. Establishing a dress code is entirely up to each organization. Some booths carry a theme that is depicted in a uniform, such as specially designed T-shirts, tuxedos or national costume. To avoid any of your representatives turning up in attire that may embarrass the organization, determine an acceptable clothing list beforehand. Personal hygiene is also extremely important. Encourage your staff to use mouthwash and breath mints regularly.

Like Actors on a Stage

From the moment the show opens to the time it closes, your staff's position in the booth is like that of actors on a stage. The visitors, like an audience, have come to see a performance. Their expectations are high, because they have invested precious time in attending. Visitors no longer wander aimlessly in exhibit halls: 76 percent of show visitors arrive with an agenda. According to the Trade Show Bureau, at least 50 percent of trade show visitors are there to see new products, services and technical developments.

ON THE SHOW FLOOR (continued)

Exhibit Selling vs. Field Selling

Exhibit selling and field selling are different and require different techniques. These differences include:

Exhibit Selling	Field Selling
1. Trade show floor is a ''level playing field''	1. Either buyer or seller has a territorial advantage
2. Time constraints	2. Time flexibility
3. Visitor attention span limited	3. More buyer concentration
4. Minimal information gathering	4. In-depth questioning
5. Quantity of prospects	5. Fewer prospects
6. Prospects come to you	6. You go to prospects
7. Limited demonstration opportunity	7. Extensive demonstration opportunity

1. The trade show floor is ''level playing field''

Both buyer and seller are on an equal footing. Neither has any territorial advantages, as they do in field sales. For example, if a buyer comes into a showroom, the seller is on familiar ground and has a distinct advantage.

2. Time is at a premium

Both the show hours and visitor's time are limited. The larger the show, the less time a visitor can spend at individual booths. Chances are that attendees have already decided who they want to spend time with and how much time they want to devote to each company. In the field there is more time devoted to each sales visit.

3. Limited attention span

The trade show floor is full of weird and wonderful things for visitors to see, hear, touch, smell and taste. They are bombarded with thousands of messages, colorful sales literature and enticing giveaways. With all this activity it is not surprising that people's concentration span is extremely limited.

In the field, there are fewer distractions to divert a prospect's attention, resulting in more concentration on the individual salesperson and the message.

4. Minimal information gathering

According to industry research, prospects spend on an average only three to five minutes at a booth. When compared with the average sales call of twenty to thirty minutes, it is not surprising that only a little information can be gathered.

5. Quantity of prospects

One of the main purposes of expositions is to offer exhibitors the opportunity to see more prospects than they could ever hope to in the field in the same amount of time.

6. Prospects come to you

At shows, prospects come to you; in the field, you, more often than not, go to them.

7. Limited demonstration opportunity

Time constraints and limited attention spans do not permit extensive demonstrations of products or services. However, shows often offer the advantage of demonstrating large equipment that would normally only be available to prospects who visited your plant or showroom.

SELLING IS SELLING

No matter where you are, on the show floor or in the field, selling is selling and buyers are buyers. Buyer concerns are constant despite the environment. Some of these concerns include whether your company is dependable and sound and if it offers a quality product or service, at a comparable value and price. Buyers will want to know if you understand their needs and will ask you why they should change. They also fear making a wrong decision.

On the show floor the three main activities are searching for and meeting prospects, questioning to discover needs, and presenting and proposing solutions. At some shows orders are taken or sales are made.

Searching for Prospects

Now all your preparation—the preshow marketing, publicity, the at-show promotion, the invitations issued, the phone calls made—comes to fruition. Is the rest fate? Definitely not! There is still plenty that can and needs to be done.

DETERMINING VISITOR TYPES

The trade show floor is full of different types of people with different agendas. Some people have specific goals for attending the show; others do not. Your observation and questioning skills will be your key to determining the following types that frequent the trade show floor:

1. **Definites.** If you have done a thorough job of preshow marketing, definite prospects and customers will visit your booth.

2. **Demonstration Junkies.** Watch out for passers-by who are attracted to your booth by a demonstration or other activity. These could be valuable prospects or time wasters. Ask a few short, open-ended questions to find out.

3. **Curiosity Cats.** These types could be curious about anything—what exactly your company does, a graphic, who designed your booth, and so on. Do not spend too much time with someone who is just interested in the design and construction of your booth or intricate details about your graphics.

4. **Paper Lovers.** Some people love to collect literature or just take any piece of paper no matter what it is. Are they attending the show to research the market for a boss? If so, they may be an influencer worth pursuing.

5. **Eyeballers.** These types are usually extremely friendly; they smile and their whole body language says, ''please talk to me.'' Questioning will determine whether or not they are prospects worth pursuing.

6. **Jeopardy Gigolos.** Winning contests is their passion. They are always ready, willing and able to drop a business card into a fishbowl for any kind of drawing. Contests that require more than just a business card to enter will help deter these types from finding their way onto your follow-up lists.

7. **Keepsakers.** Any kind of giveaway attracts these types. They may even want more than one for family, friends and colleagues. Keen questioning will ascertain if this visitor has potential.

8. **The Disinterested.** Some people in the crowd will simply not be interested in what your organization has to offer. They often let you know in no uncertain terms through their body language; for example, walking by purposely avoiding eye contact or chatting with a colleague. Waylaying these types will only upset them.

9. **Hawks.** These people attend shows for the sole purpose of selling you their products or services. Publication advertising representatives are a prime example. They are unlikely to be prospects, but you never know. If floor traffic is slow, it may be worth asking a few questions, if only to find out who they could refer you to.

SELLING IS SELLING (continued)

10. **Job Seekers.** Trade shows are an excellent place to network and look for organizations who may have present or future job openings. As with Hawks, you may want to spend time with them during slow, unproductive periods.

11. **Nonentities.** These types could be underlings in their organization sent to do some specific research. Never underestimate them. They may be extremely strong influencers. In addition, they probably know whom in their organization you need to contact. Time spent with them could be invaluable.

12. **Snoops.** Beware of the competition! These types often give themselves away by knowing too much or asking precise questions. Make sure that you do more questioning than talking so that you lessen the chances of giving away valuable information.

Understanding Customer Needs

"Treat others as they want to be treated" is the golden rule of selling. To do this requires an understanding of buyers' personalities, their focus and their basic priorities. For example, are prospects interested in technical details to influence a buying decision or are they more concerned with the bottom line? Are they reluctant to make changes or are they spontaneous decision makers?

Being able to identify a prospect's personality style will enable you to build a business relationship of trust and cooperation. It will allow you to understand a prospect's needs and wants, how they think and make decisions.

Four Personality Styles

Four personality styles and their characteristics will help you to identify customer needs and decision-making style.

1. **POWERHOUSES** are strong, forceful, outgoing, and competitive, with a great need to be in control. They are impatient, fast acting and bottom-line focused, interested in saving time and money, with little time or interest in details. They appreciate direct eye contact and a firm handshake.

2. **ENERGIZERS** are outgoing, enthusiastic, emotional, persuasive and impulsive. They love to talk but have a short attention span for listening. They seek approval from others. They are risk takers and spontaneous decision makers.

3. **DEPENDABLES** are easy-going, friendly, kind-hearted, supportive and excellent listeners. They are slow to change and need to develop a rapport of trust. Essential to their decision making are guarantees and a feeling of security.

4. **SKEPTICS** are cautious, analytical, detail-oriented, organized, persistent and accurate. They act in their own time; their decision making is based on logical and systematic data collection.

A SUMMARY OF BEHAVIORAL STYLES

	Powerhouse	Energizer
Behavior Pattern	Private Straightforward	Accessible Outspoken
Appearance	Businesslike Comfortable	Fashionable Conspicuous
Pace	Fast/Decisive	Fast/Spontaneous
Needs to Know	What it does By when What it costs	How it enhances status Who else uses it
Support Prospect's	Goals	Ideas
Likes You to Be	To the point	Stimulating
Wants to Be	In charge	Admired
Decisions Are	Definite	Spontaneous
Verbal Traits	Makes strong statements	Shares personal feelings
Vocal Traits	Forceful tone	Fast speech Dramatic
Visual Traits	Impatient Steady eye contact	Contact-oriented

Dependable	Skeptic
Accessible Uncertain	Private Diplomatic
Conventional Casual	Conservative Distinctive
Slow/Easy	Slow/Systematic
How it will affect personal circumstances	How it works How to justify the purchase logically
Feelings	Thoughts
Pleasant	Precise
Liked	Correct
Considered	Deliberate
Reserves opinions	Fact-oriented
Lower, quieter volume	Steady, monotone delivery
Patient	Few facial expressions

(*Source:* Information on personality styles is adapted from the widely-used DISC™ Model and the Personal Profile System™, copyright 1990, by Carlson Learning Company and ''Relationship Selling'' by Jim Cathcart, La Jolla, CA, Pedigree Books, 1990.)

SELLING IS SELLING (continued)

Your Behavior Style

To understand other people's personality or behavior style, it is important to identify your own style. By understanding your style and then modifyng it, you can then build rapport with your booth visitors.

Check one box in either Group 1 or Group 2 for each pair that is more like you:

Group 1	**Group 2**
☐ more controlling	☐ or more easy-going
☐ more take charge	☐ or more go along
☐ more assertive	☐ or more hesitant
☐ more challenging	☐ or more agreeable
☐ more active	☐ or more thoughtful
☐ more confronting	☐ or more understanding
☐ more talkative	☐ or more quiet
☐ more bold	☐ or more withdrawn
☐ more intense	☐ or more relaxed
☐ more forceful	☐ or more tactful
☐ more informal	☐ or more formal
☐ more spontaneous	☐ or more disciplined
☐ more responsive	☐ or more self-controlled
☐ more impulsive	☐ or more methodical
☐ more close	☐ or more distant
☐ more sensitive	☐ or more thinking
☐ more people-oriented	☐ or more task-oriented
☐ more outgoing	☐ or more reserved
☐ more dramatic	☐ or more matter-of-fact
☐ more warm	☐ or more cool

Total Group 1 column and transpose to horizontal line page 65

Total Group 2 column and transpose to vertical line page 65

Behavioral Style Matrix

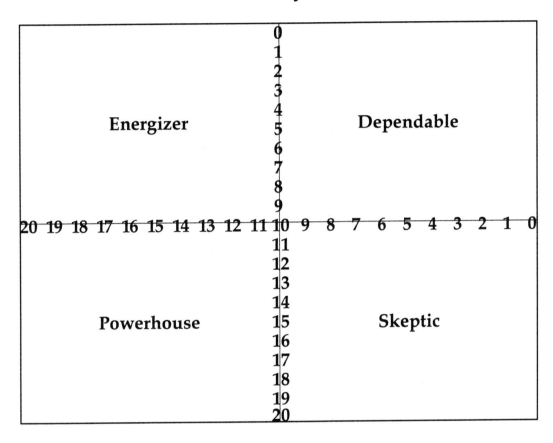

You are a *Powerhouse* if your scores fall in the following range:

    Horizontal 10–20   Vertical 10–20

You are an *Energizer* if your scores fall in the following range:

    Horizontal 10–20   Vertical 0–10

You are a *Dependable* if your scores fall in the following range:

    Horizontal 0–10   Vertical 0–10

You are a *Skeptic* if your scores fall in the following range:

    Horizontal 0–10   Vertical 10–20

If you scored 10 on both the horizontal and the vertical, you might be trying to be all things to all people.

SELLING IS SELLING (continued)

Distinguishing Personality Styles In 60 Seconds Or Less

Zeroing in on a visitor's personality style needs to be accomplished in as short a time as possible to help you build rapport. Ask yourself, "Is this person outgoing or reserved?"

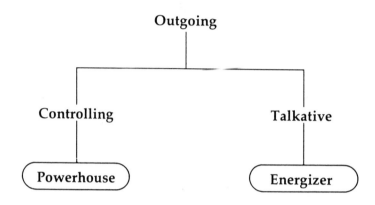

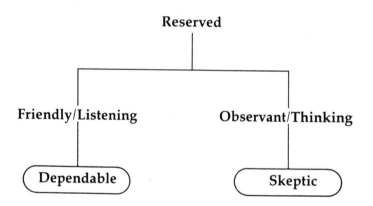

Strategies for Powerhouses: Powerhouses communicate using an outgoing, job-oriented approach. Keep the relationship professional and businesslike and avoid small talk. Be considerate of their time. Always be prepared and well-organized and get to the point quickly. Learn their goals and objectives, understand what they want to accomplish and discover what is happening now and how they want to see it changed.

Powerhouses focus on bottom-line results, not details. Ask what they want to accomplish. Ask what they want to happen that is not happening now and ask what you can do to help them save time or money.

Strategies for Energizers: Energizers communicate using an outgoing, people-oriented approach. Be very open and informal with them. Allow them time to talk, but keep them focused. Be stimulating and interested in them, use testimonials and illustrations. Be specific and stress product or service benefits that give status.

Energizers focus on *relationships* and being admired. Ask who will be involved in using the product or service. Ask what they or others in their organization like or dislike about what is presently being utilized, and ask how they feel about your product or service.

Strategies for Dependables: Dependables communicate using a restrained, people-oriented approach. Show personal interest and be likeable, friendly, professional and nonthreatening. Move at a slow pace. Develop trust, friendship and credibility with small talk. Understand their feelings as well as their technical and business needs and provide personal assurances and guarantees. Get them involved.

Dependables focus on feelings of security and trust. Ask what would help them do their jobs better and what risks you can help them avoid. Ask them what has worked well for them in the past.

Strategies for Skeptics: Skeptics communicate using a restrained, methodical approach. Be professional, formal, systematic, exact, organized and prepared to supply extensive technical data. Avoid small talk and gimmicks. Show them how it works and get them involved with a demonstration. Propose logical solutions to their problems but don't push; give them time to think.

Skeptics focus on specific and analytical professional interests. Ask for their opinions and what would help their organization run more efficiently. Ask questions that solicit facts and specific answers.

GETTING PEOPLE'S ATTENTION

Ice Breakers

With all the activity on the show floor and the thousands of messages diverting visitors' concentration, the challenge is to grab and keep their attention. What can you do to break a visitor's preoccupation?

Your opening remark, statement or question is critical in determining whether or not a visitor will want to spend time with you.

Do not ask trite questions, such as: "Can I help you?" "How are you doing today?" and "Are you enjoying the show?" These types of questions only give you the usual, standard answers that waste precious time. They are not conducive to furthering a real conversation regarding the visitor's needs.

Attention Grabbers

Questions that stop people in their tracks are not spontaneous. They need to be preplanned. Your staffers need to have three to six openers they can interchange. This will stop them sounding like a stuck record, having to repeat the same question with every visitor.

Questions should always be open-ended; that is, beginning with who, what, where, when, why or how. They stimulate thought and encourage conversation. Ask questions related to the industry, product or service and its benefits or a specific situation.

ATTENTION GRABBERS

Attention-Grabbing Questions

1. Industry-Related Questions

Sample question: ''What concerns does your organization have regarding (issue)?''

_____

_____

_____

2. Products or Service-Related Questions

Sample question: ''How could you see using a (product or service) in your organization?''

_____

_____

_____

3. Benefit-Related Questions

Sample question: ''How important is (benefit) in your present situation?''

_____

_____

_____

4. Situation-Related Questions

Sample question: ''What are your most important needs in (situation)?''

_____

_____

_____

MEETING VISITORS

Most visitors (58 percent) will wait one minute or less for a representative and 42 percent will wait three to five minutes. At peak traffic times, you may run short of representatives to meet attendees.

Amount of Time a Visitor Will Wait for a Sales Rep in a Booth

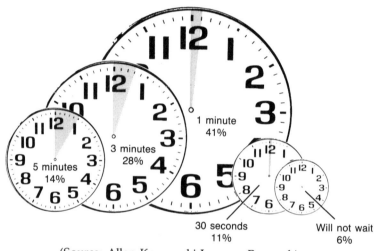

(Source: Allen Konopacki Incomm Research)

Have extra helpers available to handle routine requests for general information. Having a continuous video playing to hold prospects' attention can act as an extra sales representative.

Some types of staff behavior will deter visitors. Most attendees would feel awkward about interrupting staffers chatting together in a cozy cluster, more interested in their conversation than in the visitors.

Staffers should not stand or sit around eating, drinking or smoking. They should not read, or look bored and disinterested. Visitors view this as being highly unprofessional.

Do not leave your booth unattended. It shows a total lack of interest. Remember, people—not literature or empty booths—sell products or services. If you are exhibiting on your own, hire a temporary to relieve you every few hours. Better to have someone than no one.

QUESTIONING OR QUALIFYING PROSPECTS

The process of qualifying is one of the most important tasks, and the techniques used should be well rehearsed before the show. You need to ask questions that help build rapport in the three to five minutes.

The key to successful qualification is found in effective questioning and active listening. Whether you ask questions first and then listen, or listen first and then ask questions, these skills are the secret to successful qualification.

> **Bonus Tip:** A good probing question is: ''That's interesting. Could you tell me more about it?''

The Power of Asking Effective Questions

Many salespeople unfortunately believe the following myths:

Myth #1:   If they are not talking, they are not selling.

Myth #2:   If they are talking, they are in control.

Often, they are so excited about their product or service, they overload the prospect with information.

A true professional knows that the real skill in selling is finding the prospect's ''hot button.'' This can only be done through effective questioning and active listening. The more talking your prospect does, the more information you can gather to piece together for an effective demonstration and ultimately a sale.

You are in control of the conversation when you are asking the questions. You lead the discussion through your questioning skills.

The 80/20 Rule

When you are with a prospect, use the 80/20 rule:

80% of the time is spent listening to prospects and

20% of the time is spent talking about your products or services.

Effective questioning skills mean putting the visitor at ease, looking to build rapport. Do not bombard prospects with questions that give them the impression of being interrogated. This will only put them on the defensive. You have two ears and one mouth. They need to be used in that ratio—2:1.

MEETING VISITORS (continued)

The Power Of Active Listening

The art of active listening is important and powerful. Without it much of the dialogue that takes place between prospect and staffer can be lost, misinterpreted or misconstrued.

Active listening takes effort and intense concentration. Alessandra, Wexler and Barrera, in *Non-Manipulative Selling* (Prentice Hall Press, 1987) refer to the active listener as:

> someone who refrains from evaluating the message and tries to see the other person's point of view. Attention is not only on the words spoken but on the thoughts and feelings they convey. Listening in this way means the listener puts themself into someone else's shoes. It requires the listener to give the other person verbal and nonverbal feedback.

One of the main criteria in your team selection is to have people who are good listeners. Research indicates that most people listen with 50 percent efficiency.

Some listening habits can irritate your prospects or visitors. See which ones apply to you. Ask your team members to point out habits you may not be aware of.

20 HABITS TO AVOID

TWENTY LISTENING HABITS THAT IRRITATE PROSPECTS OR VISITORS

1. Doing all the talking

2. Interrupting when another person is talking

3. Never looking at the person talking

4. Playing with something in your hands or jangling coins in your pocket

5. Keeping a poker face so visitors do not know whether you understand them

6. Being too serious and never smiling

7. Changing what others say by putting words into their mouths

8. Occasionally asking a question about what has just been said, showing you weren't listening

9. Everything that is said reminds you of an experience you've had, and you digress with a story

10. Finishing a sentence for people if they pause too long

11. Working too hard at maintaining eye contact and making people feel uncomfortable

12. Eyeing a person up and down with nonverbal sexual connotations

13. Measuring people's words as being ''believable'' or ''unbelievable''

14. Overdoing the feedback you give—too many nods of your head or uh-huh's

15. Standing too near or far from people

16. Acting as if you know it all

17. Making judgments about people while they speak

18. Feeling obligated to listen rather than being sincerely interested in or empathetic toward the visitor

19. Being too emotionally involved in the conversation and missing the main points of the message

20. Being close-minded to someone of the opposite sex or a visitor who is younger or older than yourself

(Source: Alessandra, Wexler and Barrera. *Non-Manipulative Selling*. Prentice Hall Press, 1989)

Changing established habits takes practice and time. Awareness is the initial stage. This is an opportunity for team members to help each other.

MEETING VISTORS (continued)

Listening Work Sheet

Individual Exercise

Listening habits I am aware of:

_____

_____

_____

_____

_____

_____

Group Exercise

Listening habits I am unaware of:

_____

_____

_____

_____

_____

_____

What actions do I need to take to overcome these habits?

_____

_____

_____

_____

_____

_____

PRESENTING OR DEMONSTRATING TO YOUR PROSPECTS

Some principles apply to all demonstrations. Learn how everything works before the show, and every day before the show opening, check that everything is working. List all the strong features of the products or services; learn the benefits attached to the features. List all the areas where you can involve the prospect and show them what to do. Allow them to try to assist in the process. When you talk to a prospect, use positive pauses to increase credibility and persuasive eye contact. Always ask open questions and be prepared, anticipate questions.

The FBI Principle of Presenting

When you present your product or service to a prospect, think of its features, how it will benefit the customer and what the customer thinks of it.

F **Feature**, a characteristic of your product or service that will meet the prospect's needs. For example, computer software with pull-down menus.

B **Benefit**, a value obtained from the product or service. For example, saving time accessing important data.

I **Inclination**, the prospect's opinion. For example, "How do you feel this will satisfy your need for simplifying repetitive tasks?"

By using the FBI principle of presenting, you state product or service features supported by benefits that you know from your previous questioning are important to the prospect. Then you ask for the prospect's opinion. This method keeps the prospect involved and interested.

Bonus Tip: To test if a benefit is a true benefit, ask yourself: "What will it do for the prospect?"

PRESENTING TO DIFFERENT PERSONALITY TYPES

Presenting to the different personality types calls for different techniques.

Presenting to Powerhouses

► Be brief and to the point

► Avoid technical information unless requested

► Talk benefits, emphasizing saving time and money

Presenting to Energizers

► Avoid technical information

► Make them feel good and have fun

► Stress status and recognition-oriented benefits

Presenting to Dependables

► Beware of information overload

► Stress benefits that stabilize, simplify or support their situation

► Provide guarantees and personal assurances

Presenting to Skeptics

► Show logical proof from specific sources

► Allow them to share their knowledge and expertise

► Emphasize quality, value and reliability

PRESENTING PREPARATION EXERCISE

In which areas can prospects be involved?

_____

_____

_____

_____

_____

What are the strongest features and benefits of our product or service?

Feature: _____

Benefit: _____

Feature: _____

Benefit: _____

Feature: _____

Benefit: _____

Feature:

Benefit: _____

What questions can we anticipate?

_____

_____

_____

_____

INFORMATION NEEDED TO QUALIFY PROSPECTS

The following 10 areas need to be covered during the conversation with your prospect. Remember that each personality style needs a different approach.

1. Their name and position in the company

2. The company they represent

3. Problems they are looking to solve

4. The needs that exist for your product or service

5. Plans for using your product or service

6. Product or service presently being used

7. Changes in their organization to warrant the purchase of your product or service

8. The quantity needed

9. The influence or authority the visitor has in decision-making

10. The resources available for purchasing

11. The time frame for making a purchasing decision

12. Knowing when the company plans its budget

Bonus Tip: Find out immediately who the prospect is and where they are from. You do not want to spend unnecessary time with someone outside your distribution area.

THE LEAD CARD

Information that is gathered needs to be recorded on an easy-to-use sales lead card similar to the one shown below. Trying to commit information to memory or scribbling undecipherable notes on the back of business cards is not effective.

Properly qualified leads reduce costs. According to the Trade Show Bureau, for 54 percent of orders placed after a show, a personal sales visit is not required. Closing costs for qualified leads are almost 70 percent less than sales without leads. (The average sales call costs $259, whereas the average trade show lead costs $142.)

SAMPLE LEAD CARD

Show: _____ Date: _____

Prospect name: _____

Title and Company: _____

Address: _____

City: _____ State: _____ Zip: _____

Phone: _____ Fax: _____

Product or service presently used: _____

Products or services of interest: _____

Level of interest: ☐ excellent ☐ fair ☐ poor ☐ unknown

Decision-making influence/process: ☐ sole decision maker ☐ group decision
☐ committee ☐ influencer ☐ none ☐ other: _____

Purchasing time frame: _____

Comments: _____

Booth representative: _____

Bonus Tip: For high traffic shows when you know it will be impossible to speak to everyone, consider having a contest that requires a prequalification. Develop an entry form with three to five prequalifying questions.

THE IMPORTANCE OF NONVERBAL COMMUNICATION

Prospects can give us plenty of information about themselves through their body language, handshakes, hand and arm gestures and face and eye contact. In a five-minute interaction with a prospect more than 200 nonverbal messages could be exchanged.

According to Albert Mehrabian, researcher in the field of nonverbal communication (UCLA), communication is 7 percent words, 38 percent tone of voice and 55 percent body language. It is not what we say, but rather how we say it.

There is nothing like a good firm handshake to inspire confidence. But some handshakes create other feelings:

- *Palm-down thrust.* Typical of an aggressive, dominant male who forces the other person's palm into his, with his on top, denoting control.

- *Glove or politician's handshake.* The prospect envelopes your hand with both his hands. A gesture of trust and honesty is implied, but the reverse is felt—disbelief and caution about the person's real intentions. This handshake should only be used with existing prospects and customers.

- *Elbow grasp.* They grasp your hand with one hand and your elbow with the other. Like the glove, it is considered too intimate for a first meeting and denotes suspicion and mistrust.

- *Dead fish.* A cold, clammy, limp handshake is associated with a weak character or someone who is bored and disinterested.

- *Finger-tip grab.* The initiator misses the hand and just catches the other person's fingers. Even if there is an enthusiastic attitude, this person lacks confidence.

(Source: Pease, Allan. *Silent Signals.* Bantam Books)

INTERPRETING BODY LANGUAGE

You can tell how your prospects feel by how they behave. You can get more out of your encounter if you understand basic body language. If the prospect exhibits:

Power and Superiority	*Will be displayed as:* unwavering eye contact, a strong, palm-down handshake, hands on hips or in pockets with exposed thumbs, steepled fingers
Nervousness	*Will be displayed as:* inability to maintain eye contact, blinks often, purse or briefcase placed in front of body, shifting from foot to foot, fidgeting, pen clicking
Skepticism	*Will be displayed as:* arms folded across chest, squinting eyes, fingers adjusting collar, scowling, body angled to speaker
Boredom or Disinterest	*Will be displayed as:* Staring into space, jingling objects in pockets or hands, looking at watch, picks at or adjusts clothing, taps or jiggles foot
Suspicion or Dishonesty	*Will be displayed as:* avoiding eye contact, glancing sideways, hands near or touching nose, ears, or mouth while speaking, gestures not matching words, body poised to move away

THE IMPORTANCE OF NONVERBAL COMMUNICATION (continued)

Uncertainty and Indecision

Will be displayed as:

closed eyes while pinching bridge of nose, chewing or biting lip, sideways eye movement, pacing, looks concerned or puzzled, slight tilt of head

Evaluation

Will be displayed as:

Hand on or stroking chin with index finger prominent, slightly tilted head, index finger on lips, eyeglasses or pen in mouth, ear turned toward speaker

If you want to express confidence to your prospect, stand with your feet about a foot apart, your arms at your side and shoulders relaxed. Stand 1.5'–4' away from your prospect, and do not have any object covering the front of your body. Shake hands in a vertical (straight up and down) position, and always smile and look welcoming.

TECHNIQUES FOR ENDING A CONVERSATION

The time has come to close your conversation and bid your prospect farewell. Often the conversation will come to a natural close, but there are times when your prospect is not in a hurry to leave. The use of specific body language and well-prepared closing statements will give your prospect a clear message.

Use the prospect's name. First, change your body position and shake hands. Then communicate your follow-up action plan. Last, give your prospect a gift or token for taking time to stop. If you do these and minimize your eye contact, the prospect will get the message.

What to Do with the Time-Waster Visitor

Occasionally, you have a visitor who is wasting your time or you discover the competition snooping around. You want to quickly encourage both to leave your booth. You can do this politely by saying: *"I appreciate your stopping at our booth. From our conversation, it doesn't appear that we can be of service to you at this time. If your situation changes, please feel free to contact me. Here's my card."*

Shake their hand and get rid of them, because during the time you are spending with them, several potentially good prospects could be passing you by.

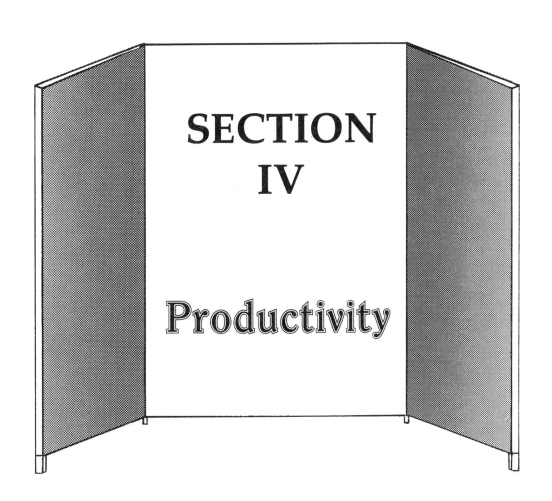

SECTION
IV

Productivity

PRODUCTIVITY

Once the show is over, the real business begins—following up all the leads and filling the visitor requests. The biggest mistake exhibitors make is not having a plan of action to follow up their hundreds of trade show leads. They are usually just given out to the sales force and left to take care of themselves.

What often happens is that these leads are a low priority for the salespeople and are left for weeks or months before contact is made. Or, the sales representative tries to contact the trade show prospect to set up an appointment and becomes frustrated at the number of calls it takes to reach the person. Once a connection is made, they discover the prospect has no real interest at this time, they need to be speaking to someone else, or the competition has already made the sale.

Most exhibitors fail to realize two important factors: first, that follow-up timing is critical and, second, that not all leads can be handled in the same way. The key is to make the follow-up process easy and efficient, so that the main focus is on finalizing the sale.

TURNING TRADE SHOW LEADS AND INQUIRIES INTO SALES

Send a letter to all show visitors. Create a "thank you for visiting our booth" letter before leaving for the show. Include your intention to follow up within the next week.

At the end of each show, overnight or fax your show inquiries to your office for the letters to be sent out, and establish a system to facilitate the mailing. Timing is critical. Your letters need to reach prospects within 48 hours after the show has ended, because you want to keep your company name in their minds. Once back at their office, prospects easily forget what they saw, did or said at the show.

> **Bonus Tip:** Award a prize to everyone who entered your contest to initiate another contact with the visitor.

Evaluate your inquiries. Group your inquiries into categories guided by the "level of interest" response on the lead card. For example: A = Excellent prospects, B = Good prospects, C = Fair prospects, D = Poor prospects, E = Hard to assess.

These prospects now need to be requalified over the phone. This is the most cost-effective way to establish their true interest before handing the leads over to the sales representatives.

Develop a telephone qualification questionnaire, which should be prepared before the show. It needs to be short and to the point, so that it takes only several minutes to be completed. Include an introductory message, questions relating to the prospect's need for your product or service, time-frame and budget-related questions, their decision-making process and any action to be taken.

SAMPLE QUESTIONNAIRE

Sample Telephone Qualification Questionnaire

Good morning, I'm _____ with _____ . I'm following up the interest you expressed about our product/service at the recent _____ trade show.

At the show you (restate a need they expressed at the show that appears on the lead card).

Could you help me understand your situation better? Tell me . . .

1. Are you presently using a similar product or service? ☐ Yes ☐ No

   (If yes) Are you considering purchasing another product or service? ☐ Yes ☐ No

   (If no) Are you interested in purchasing a (product or service)? ☐ Yes ☐ No
   (If answer is "no," thank them for their time and terminate the conversation.)

2. What are the major reasons for considering a purchase of this nature?

   _____

3. Within what period of time will a purchasing decision be made?

   ☐ 1 month   ☐ 3 months   ☐ 6 months   ☐ other: _____

4. Has a budget for this product or service been allocated? ☐ Yes ☐ No

5. Are you the person who would select the supplier for this item? ☐ Yes ☐ No

   If no, who is? _____

   a) How can (person stated) be reached?

   Phone number: _____ Ext. _____

   Best time to call: _____

6. Would you be interested in speaking to our representative about your specific needs?

   ☐ Yes   ☐ No   ☐ Send literature

   ☐ Other action to be taken: _____

Thank you very much for your time and cooperation.

* * *

Telephone interviewer: _____ Date contacted: _____

TURNING TRADE SHOW LEADS AND
INQUIRIES INTO SALES (continued)

Select personnel to do telephone interviews. These people need to have a good attitude toward using the phone. They must be pleasant to listen to with good voice tone, pitch and clarity. They should express themselves well and be excellent listeners. Moreover, they should have a sense of fun and not fear rejection.

Give priority to A's and B's. If you only have a couple of people available to conduct the phone interviews, give priority to the excellent (A) and the good (B) prospects. Then have your staff work through the lead cards systematically.

Plan your time frame. Complete your calls within a week after the show. Allow extra time to make contact with people. Often it can take six or more attempts to connect with the prospect.

Rate your responses. Once all the interviews have been conducted, rate your responses. For example:

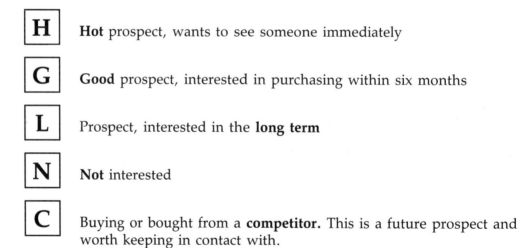

H — **Hot** prospect, wants to see someone immediately

G — **Good** prospect, interested in purchasing within six months

L — Prospect, interested in the **long term**

N — **Not** interested

C — Buying or bought from a **competitor.** This is a future prospect and worth keeping in contact with.

Once the responses are rated, note what changes in classification have emerged, from the rating on the trade show lead card to the telephone qualification rating.

Plan a method to measure sales results. Before handing the telephone qualified leads over to the sales force, organize a system to track their success rate. This could be in the form of a report after a certain period of time.

Distribute the leads. Now you have some really good qualified leads to pass on to your sales representatives. The ''hot'' and ''good'' prospects need to be followed up immediately. Send information to everyone who requested it. Keep the ''competitor'' prospects on file for future follow up.

Make your sales force accountable, because they will perform better than those who are not made accountable. Have them tell you what is a manageable number of leads they can handle in a given period of time. Allocate that number to them and have them request more as needed.

Finally, explore the lead-management computer software packages presently on the market. Investing in one could simplify this whole process.

(Source for leads to sales information: Richard Erschik, Leads to Sales, Inc., Carol Stream, IL)

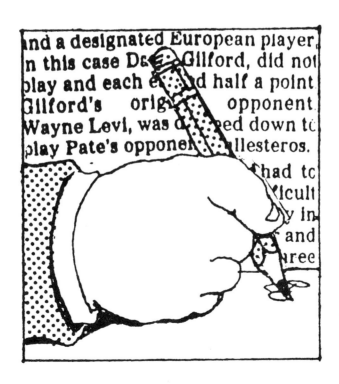

MEASURE YOUR PRODUCTIVITY

With an established lead management system you can now accurately measure the results of your trade show efforts. For example:

- **Cost per sale**—divide the total expenditure by the number of sales.

- **Cost per trade show lead**—divide total trade show expenditure by the number of trade show leads gathered.

- **Cost per telephone lead**—divide total expenditure by the number of hot, good and long-term leads.

Evaluate Your Performance

Take time to evaluate your show's performance with your booth staff. Ask the following questions:

1. How did we perform in relation to our goals?

   _____

   _____

2. What would we do differently next time we exhibit?

   _____

   _____

3. What were our challenges?

   _____

   _____

4. What happened that we did not expect?

   _____

   _____

5. In which areas do we need more preparation?

   _____

   _____

6. How effective was our booth display?

   _____

7. What changes could be made to improve our booth display?

   _____

   _____

8. Which of our products or services attracted the most attention?

   _____

   _____

9. How effective was the staffing schedule and what changes need to be made?

   _____

   _____

10. How effective was this particular show for our purposes?

    _____

    _____

11. How did the quality of visitors rate in relation to our needs?

    _____

    _____

12. Should we exhibit at this show again? If no, why?

    _____

    _____

13. Which of our competitors were also exhibiting?

    _____

    _____

14. What areas do we need to bring to show management's attention?

    _____

    _____

EVALUATE THE SHOW

After three or six months, assess how cost-effective the show was for your organization. Based on your show's productivity measurement, you can determine its cost-effectiveness for your show goals.

> **Bonus Tip:** If a show is only marginally profitable, consider whether you need to participate for offensive or defensive reasons. Think what your competitors and prospects would think of your absence.

You Have Everything You Need

Do you have the desire, commitment and discipline to plan for your shows and then work your plans? Whether you are a one-person operation or a multinational corporation, you now have the essential tools and techniques to exhibit successfully and profitably at trade shows. The rest is up to you.

The step-by-step approach of this book outlines the areas that need attention. Successful exhibiting needs a plan that starts at least nine months in advance of the show. It then requires attention to details and deadlines. For every minute of planning you save five minutes in execution. Plans put together at the eleventh hour are doomed to failure.

Being a smart exhibitor means having specific goals and a strategy. Have one person take on the overall responsibility for managing your exhibit, supported by a team of committed employees. They need to meet regularly to ensure deadlines and issues are met.

Select a team whom you are proud to have represent you and include them in planning the show. This helps to keep them interested and committed to the project, and they will feel more accountable to you and the show. Ensure they have the skills to do the job that is expected of them.

Let your customers, clients, suppliers, distributors, et al know that you are exhibiting and where to find you. Remember that nothing will happen as a result of the show, however outstanding your performance was, unless you follow up.

Finally, learn from experience: observe other exhibitors, learn from them and duplicate what works well for them. Chances are it will work well for you, too.

> *Good Luck as a Successful and Profitable Exhibitor!*

EXHIBITOR CHECKLIST

101 Winning Ways to Increase Your Trade Show Success

Are you getting the best return on your show investment? This checklist acts as a reminder for many of the questions covered in this book that you need to ask before participating in a trade or consumer show. Your answers will help ensure that your participation is a professional one.

ON YOUR MARK . . .

1. Why am I exhibiting?

2. What am I exhibiting?

3. Who is my target audience?

4. How well does this show fit my marketing needs?

5. How convenient are the show dates?

6. What else is happening on those dates?

7. How convenient is the show location?

8. Will the show attract prospects my company can service?

9. How accessible is the show location?

10. Is there ample parking at the show site?

11. How successful has this show been in the past?

12. How experienced are show management in organizing this type of show?

13. What are show management doing to promote the show?

14. Will show management give me a list of previous exhibitors to contact about the show?

15. How do show management work with show labor?

16. How sympathetic is show management to exhibitor problems?

17. Do I have a written exhibition plan?

18. Have I established an exhibiting budget (including additional costs)?

EXHIBITOR CHECKLIST (continued)

> *GET SET . . .*

19. Have I thoroughly read and understood the contract?

20. Have I reserved my site?

21. Have I paid the necessary deposit?

22. Have I planned the booth design?

23. Do I have the right amount of space?

24. Is there room for display units, furnishings, demonstrations?

25. Can visitors move about freely without overcrowding?

26. Have I ordered: signage, floor covering, sufficient lighting, electricity, plumbing, air, water, drainage, audio visual equipment, plants or floral decorations and booth cleaning services?

27. Have I appointed a booth manager?

28. Have I planned my staff requirements, including extras in case of illness or emergency?

29. Have I selected the booth personnel?

30. Does my staff require training?

31. Have I organized a preshow meeting?

32. Is the booth team knowledgeable about the products and services that will be displayed?

33. Can they demonstrate them effectively?

34. Will someone be available to answer technical questions?

35. Do I need literature, catalogs or price lists printed?

36. Have press kits been prepared?

37. Have any other PR opportunities been arranged?

38. Do I need to plan a special feature or celebrity?

39. Have I sent the organizers information for my show guide entry?

40. Do I want to organize any peripheral advertising (such as trade publications, radio, TV)?

41. Have I organized any promotional giveaways?

42. Has a visitor competition been organized?

43. Is our competition or giveaway in line with state lottery laws?

44. Have I ordered enough tickets?

45. Have I ordered badges for all the staff personnel?

46. Has a ticket distribution system been organized?

47. Should personal invitations be sent to customers or prospects?

48. Is labor needed for booth installation and dismantling?

49. Do I need to make arrangements to ship freight?

50. Have I mailed a copy of my freight instructions to the show contractor?

51. Have I mailed a copy of my freight instructions to my booth manager?

52. Are there any union restrictions I need to know?

53. Have I arranged insurance?

54. Are security arrangements necessary?

55. Has a tool kit been put together?

56. Have the necessary hotel arrangements been made?

GO!

57. Has final payment been sent for booth space?

58. Does our booth meet our objectives?

59. Does the exhibit structure look inviting to visitors?

60. Is there an improvement that I should consider?

61. Have I informed my staff of all the pertinent building rules and regulations?

62. Am I motivating my staff about their important role at the show?

63. Has a practice mock-up session including demonstrations been organized and held?

64. Do all the booth personnel have business cards?

65. Have the necessary sales and office supplies been assembled?

66. Is a computer needed for the exhibit?

67. If so, has it been ordered?

68. Are credit card services needed for booth sales?

69. Is a vendor's license needed?

70. If so, has it been ordered?

71. Is visitor hospitality needed?

72. Has a hospitality venue been organized?

73. Is a bartender or hostess necessary?

74. Has someone been appointed to keep the booth looking neat and tidy?

75. Has a lead-taking system been organized for visitor requests?

EXHIBITOR CHECKLIST (continued)

76. Has someone been assigned to oversee the booth dismantling?

77. Does that person understand the move-out procedure?

78. Has the staff been informed on the proper closing regulations?

FINISH LINE . . .

79. Has a checklist of exhibit items been prepared to check off items as they are packed?

80. Has a critique session been organized immediately after the show?

81. Has an "after the show" follow-up system been organized for literature requests and sales calls?

82. Should a letter of thanks be sent to every registered visitor?

83. Will all leads be sent to sales people in the field for follow up?

84. Who will be responsible for doing this?

85. Who will check with the field people to see how the leads have been handled and requests processed?

86. How will sales from the show be monitored?

87. Do I want to create a mailing list from the inquiry cards?

88. Who will be responsible for producing a show report?

89. After what period will this be done?

90. Will the completed report be sent to management and sales people who did not participate in the show?

91. What kind of reward or recognition will the exhibit staff receive?

92. Who will assess whether we want to participate in the show again next year?

93. Who will be responsible for reserving our space for next year?

94. When is the earliest that reservations for next year can be made?

95. What feedback has been given to show management?

96. Did we manage to stay within the estimated show budget?

97. Does the budget need revising for next year?

98. Should we consider enlarging our display or space next year?

99. Who will be responsible for evaluating our show performance?

100. Who will be responsible for making a list of changes for the next show?

101. At which other shows should we consider exhibiting?

(Copyright 1991: Diadem Communications, Cincinnati, OH)

EXHIBITOR RESOURCES

Organizations

American Society of Association
   Executives
1575 Eye Street, Northwest
Washington, DC 20005
(202) 626-2723

Canadian Association of Exposition
   Managers
405 The West Mall, Suite 700
Etobicoke, Ontario M9C 5J1
(416) 620-6876

Exhibit Designers and Producers
   Association
611 East Wells Street
Milwaukee, WI 53202
(414) 276-3372

Exhibit Surveys, Inc.
P.O. Box 327
Middletown, NJ 07748
(201) 741-3170

Exposition Service Contractors
   Association
Union Station, Suite 210
400 South Houston Street
Dallas, TX 75202
(214) 742-9217

Health Care Exhibitors Association
5775 Peachtree-Dunwoody Road
Suite 500-D
Atlanta, GA 30342
(404) 252-3663

International Association of
   Convention and Visitors Bureaus
P.O. Box 758
Champaign, IL 61820
(217) 359-8881

International Association of Fairs
   & Expositions
P.O. Box 985
Springfield, MO 65801
(417) 862-5771

International Exhibitors Association
5103-B Backlick Road
Annandale, VA 22003
(703) 941-3725

Major American Trade Show
   Organizers
Marvin Park & Associates
600 Talcott Road
Park Ridge, IL 60068
(708) 823-2151

Meeting Planners International
INFOMART
1950 Stemmons Freeway, Suite 5018
Dallas, TX 75207
(214) 746-5222

National Association of Exposition
   Managers
719 Indiana Avenue
Indianapolis, IN 46202
(317) 638-6236

Professional Convention
   Management Association
100 Vestavia Office Park, Suite 220
Birmingham, AL 35216
(205) 823-7262

Trade Show Bureau
1660 Lincoln Street, Suite 2080
Denver, CO 80264
(303) 860-7626

EXHIBITOR RESOURCES (continued)

Publications

Creative
37 West 39th Street
New York, NY 10018
(212) 840-0160

Exhibit Builder
Sound Publishing Company
P.O. Box 920
Great Neck, NY 11022
(800) 356-4451

Exhibitor
745 Marquette Bank Building
Rochester, MN 55903
(507) 289-6556

Exhibit Marketing Magazine
Eaton Hall Publishing
123 Columbia Turnpike
Florham Park, NJ 07932
(201) 514-5900

IDEAS
International Exhibitors Association
5103-B Backlick Road
Annandale, VA 22003
(703) 941-3725

Meeting Manager
Meeting Planners International
INFOMART
1950 Stemmons Freeway, Suite 5018
Dallas, TX 75207
(214) 746-5222

Potentials in Marketing
Lakewood Publications, Inc.
50 South Ninth Street
Minneapolis, MN 55402
(612) 333-0471

Sales & Marketing Management
633 Third Avenue
New York, NY 10017
(212) 986-4800

Sales and Marketing Strategies & News
Hughes Communications, Inc.
P.O. Box 197
Rockford, IL 61105
(815) 963-4000

Successful Meetings
633 Third Avenue
New York, NY 10017
(212) 986-4800

TradeShow & Exhibit Manager
Goldstein & Associates, Inc.
1150 Yale Street, Suite 12
Santa Monica, CA 90403
(213) 828-1309

Tradeshow Week
12233 West Olympic Blvd.
Los Angeles, CA 90064
(213) 826-5696

ABOUT THE FIFTY-MINUTE SERIES

We hope you enjoyed this book and found it valuable. If so, we have good news for you. This title is part of the best selling *FIFTY-MINUTE Series* of books. All *Series* books are similar in size and format, and identical in price. Several are supported with training videos. These are identified by the symbol **v** next to the title.

Since the first *FIFTY-MINUTE* book appeared in 1986, millions of copies have been sold worldwide. Each book was developed with the reader in mind. The result is a concise, high quality module written in a positive, readable self-study format.

FIFTY-MINUTE Books and Videos are available from your distributor. A free current catalog is available on request from Crisp Publications, Inc., 95 First Street, Los Altos, CA 94022.

Following is a complete list of *FIFTY-MINUTE Series* Books and Videos organized by general subject area.

Management Training (continued):

Personal Improvement:

Human Resources & Wellness:

Small Business & Financial Planning:

Adult Literacy & Learning:

Career/Retirement & Life Planning: